Vol 12

MAZE

FOR KIDS

Ages 4-6

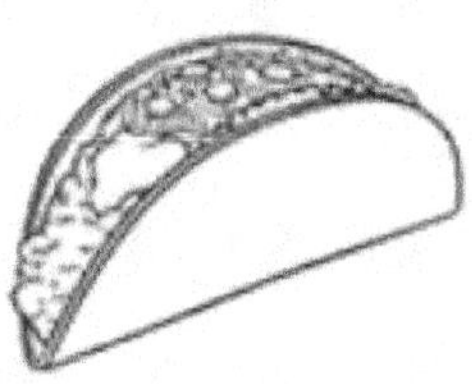

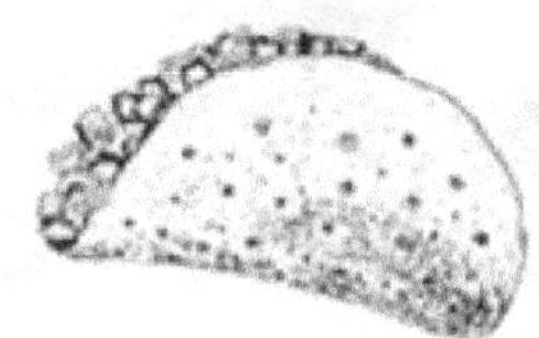

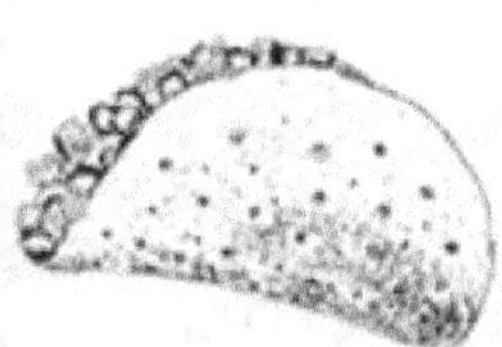

MAZE BOOK

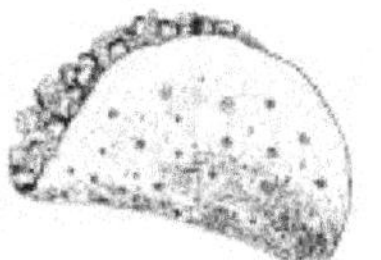

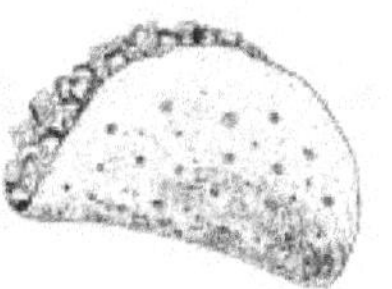

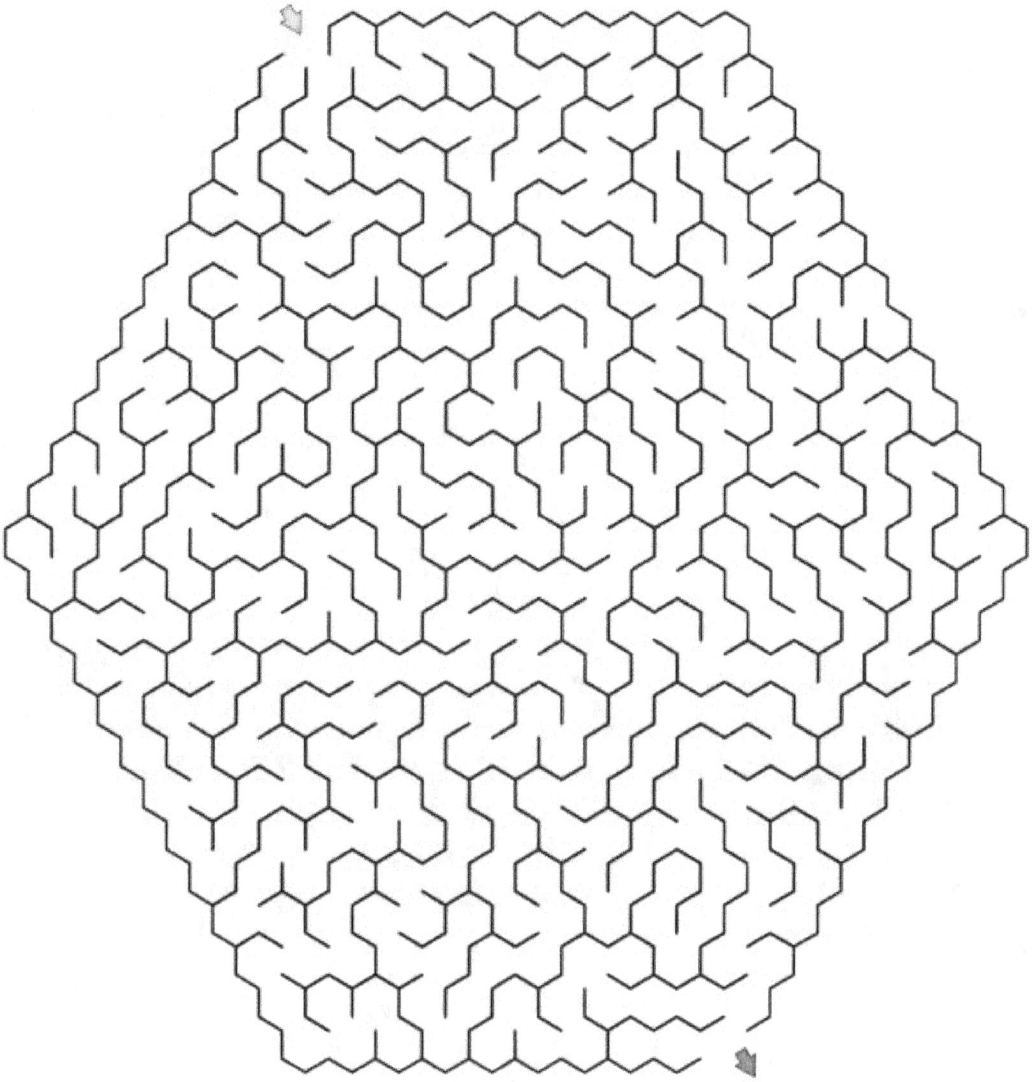

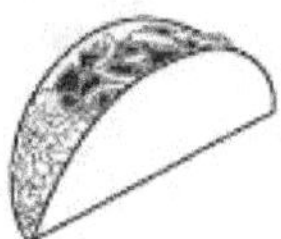

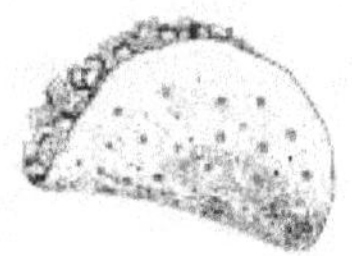

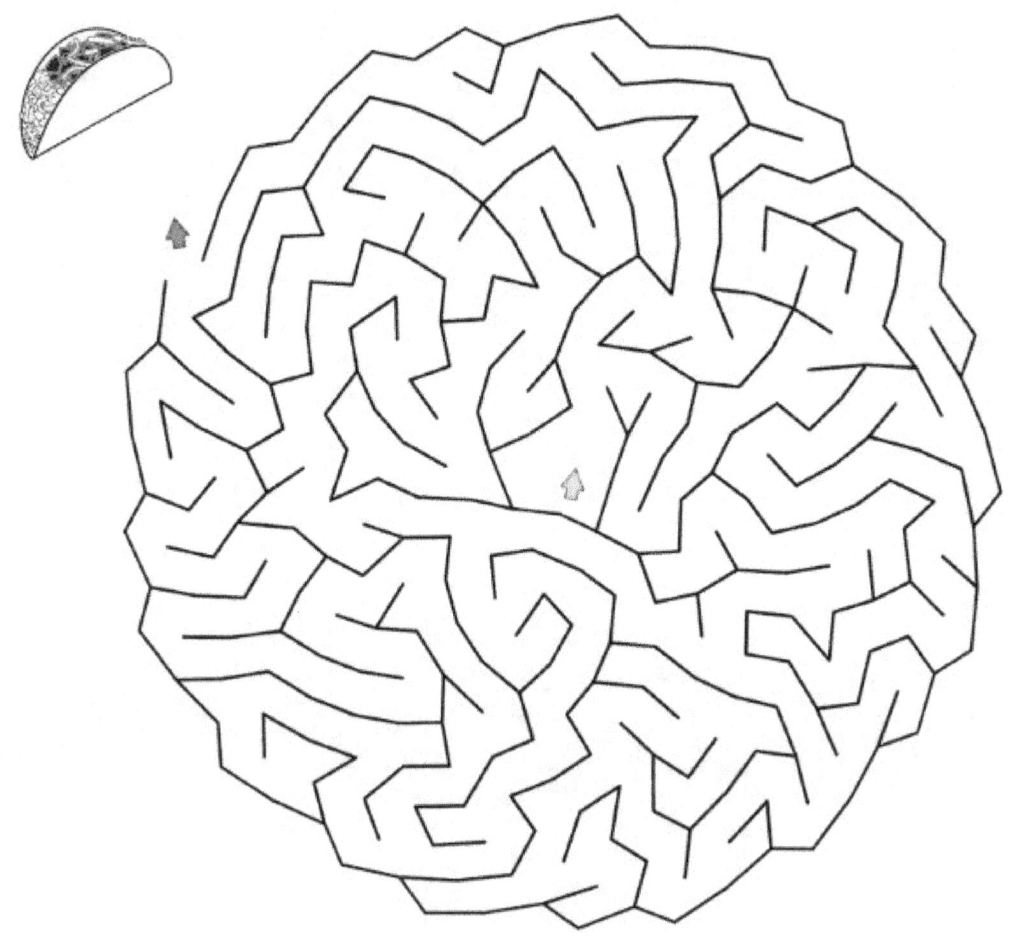

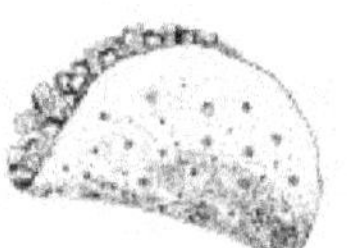

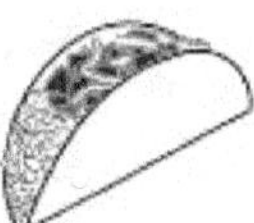

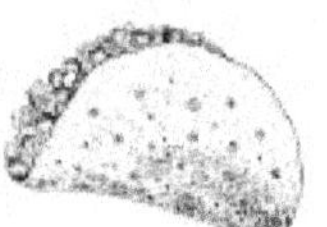

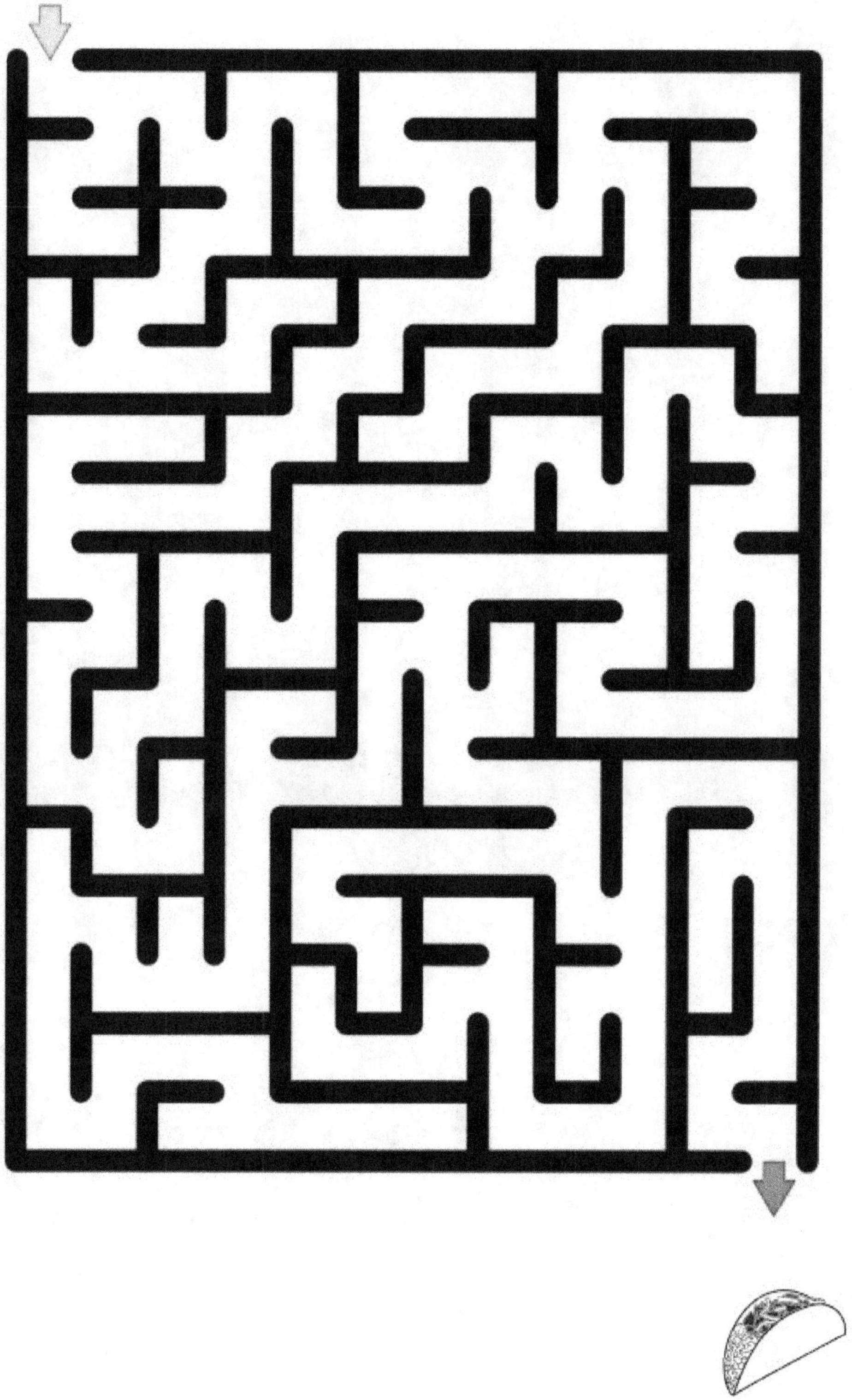

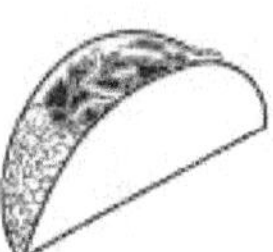

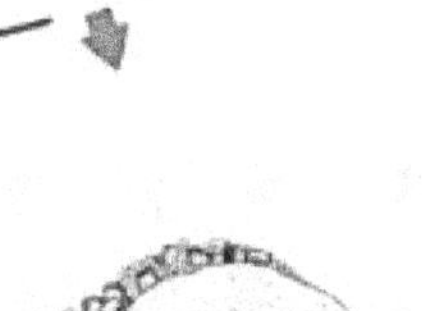

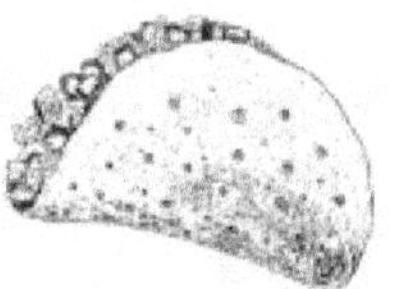

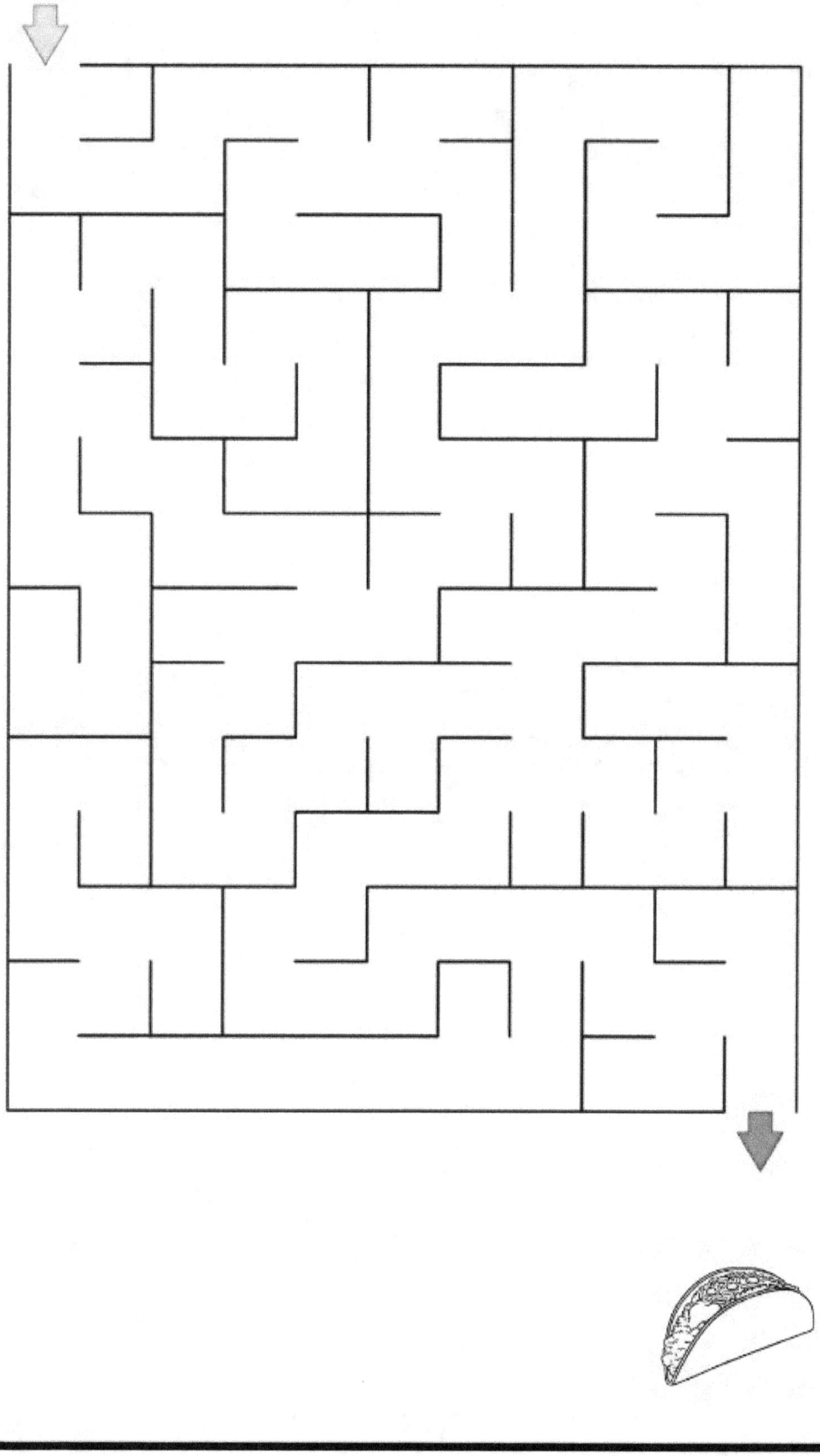

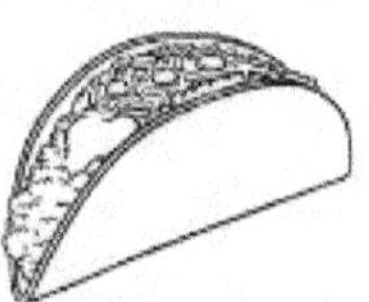

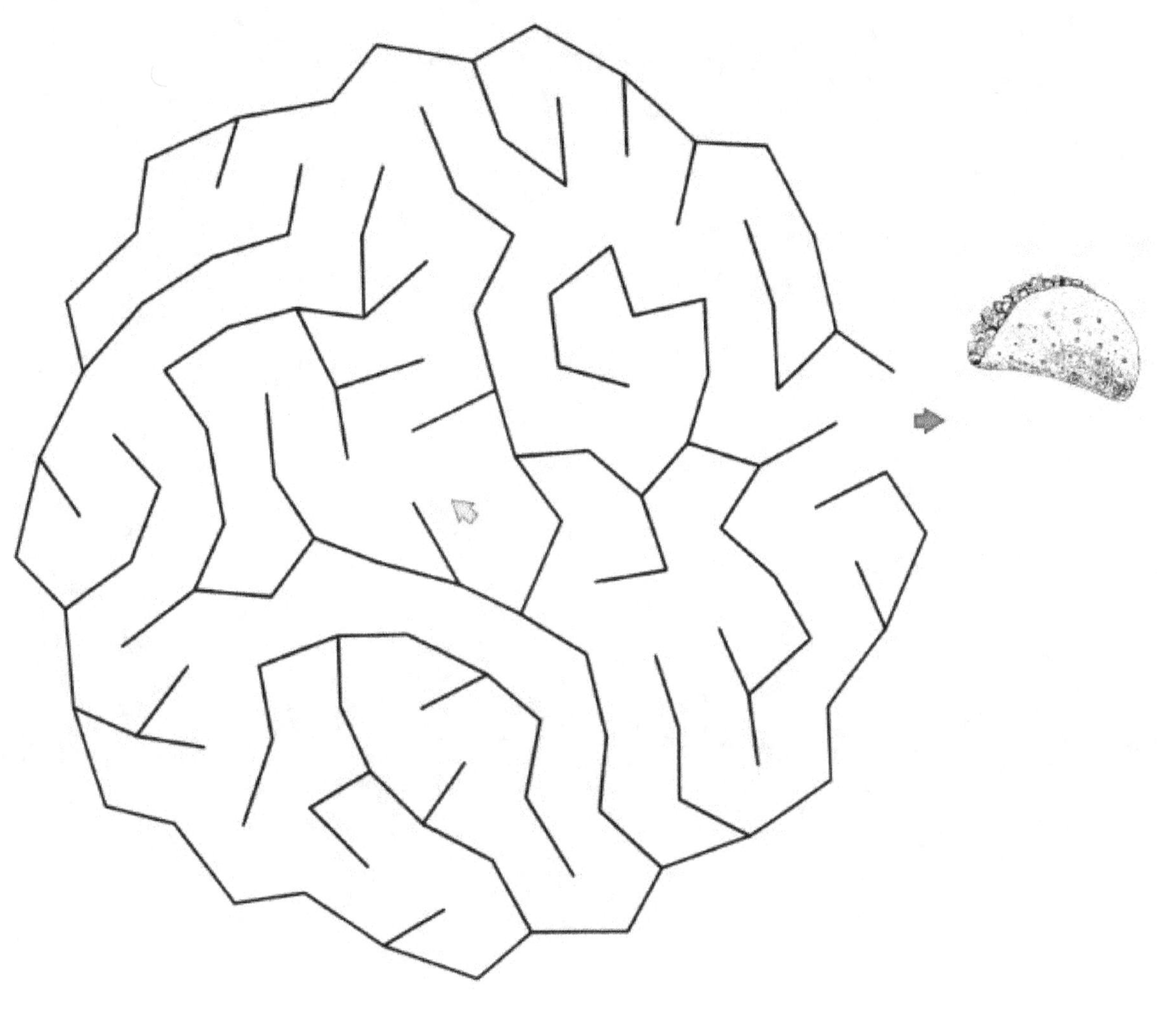

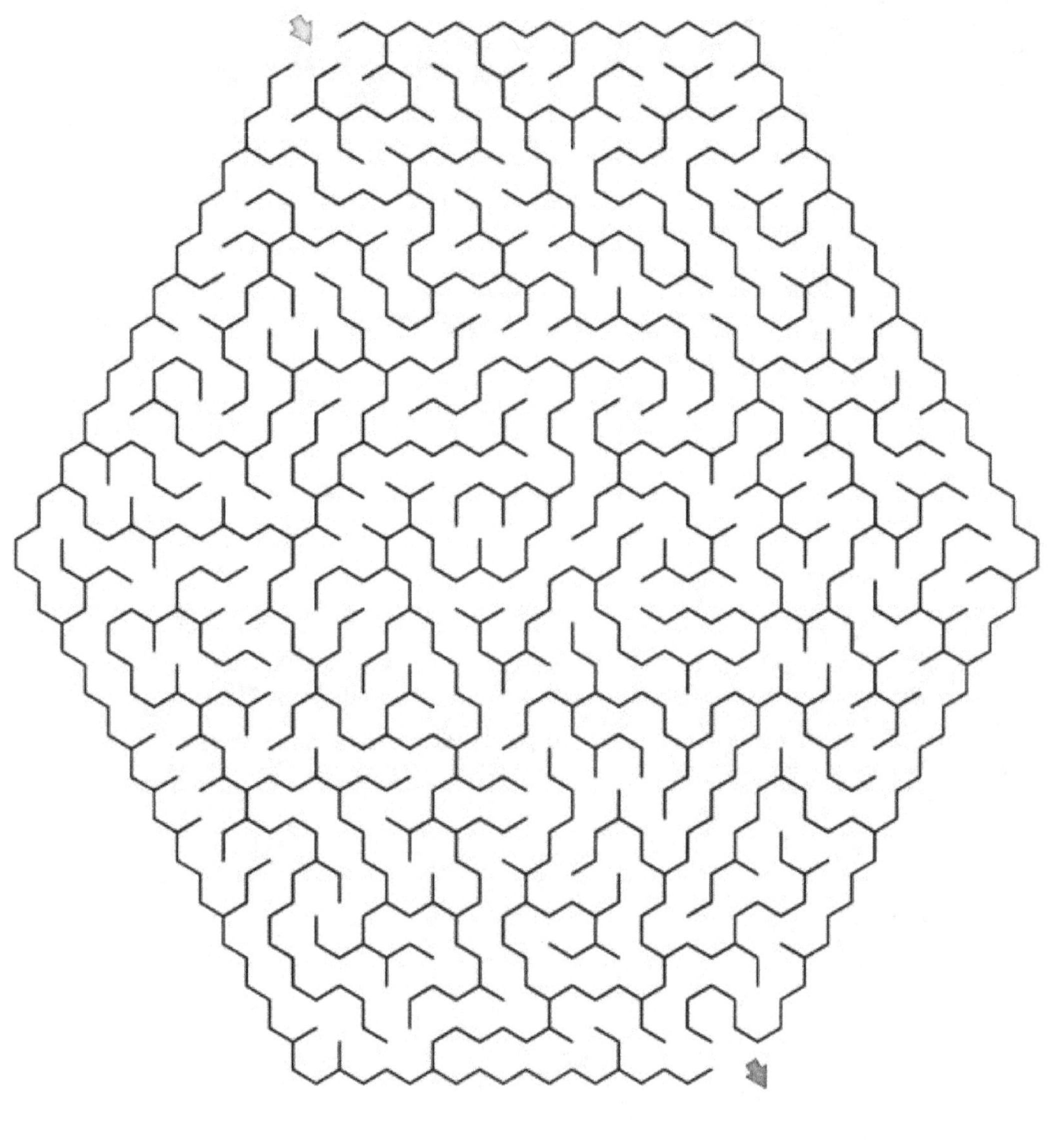

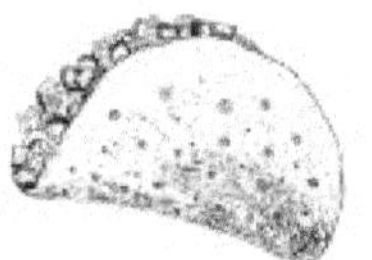

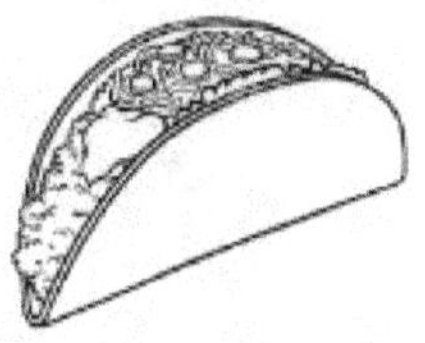

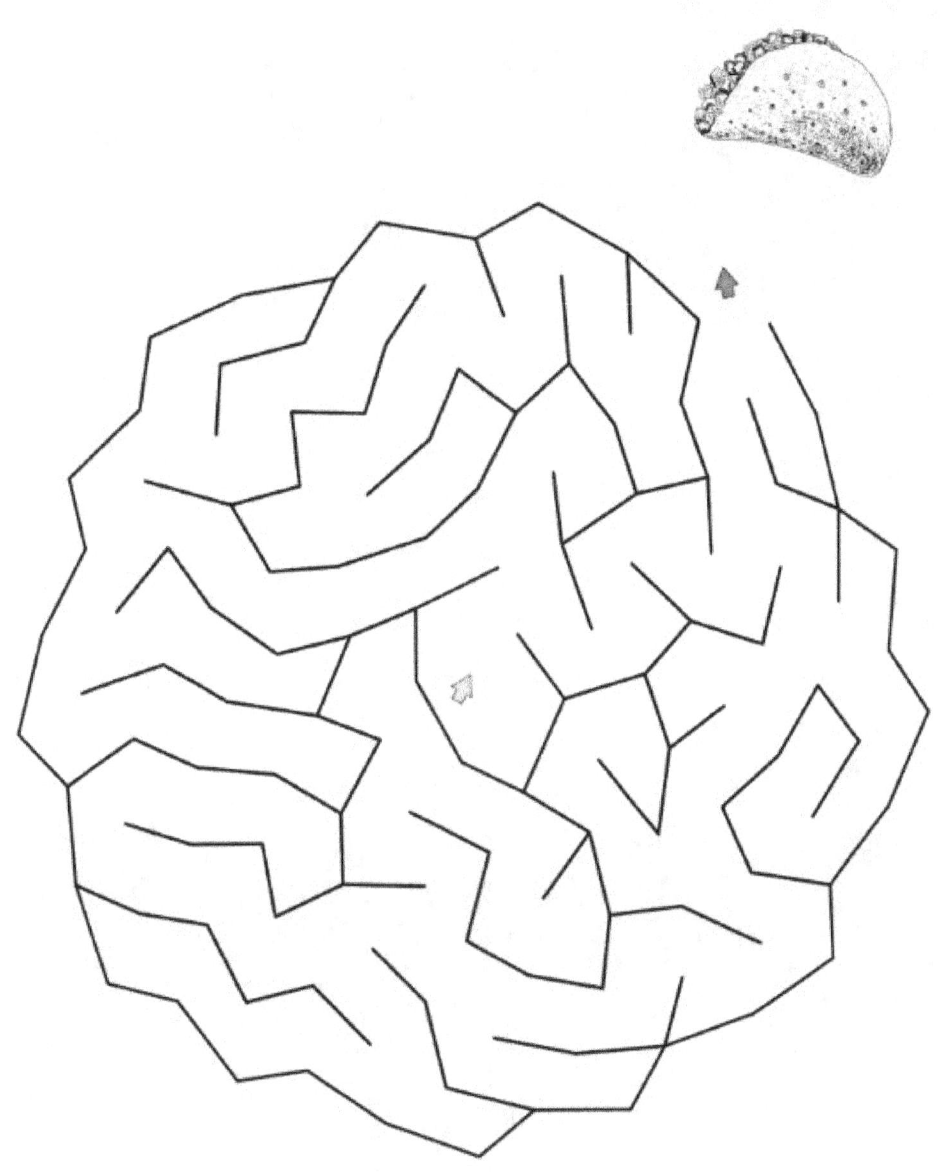

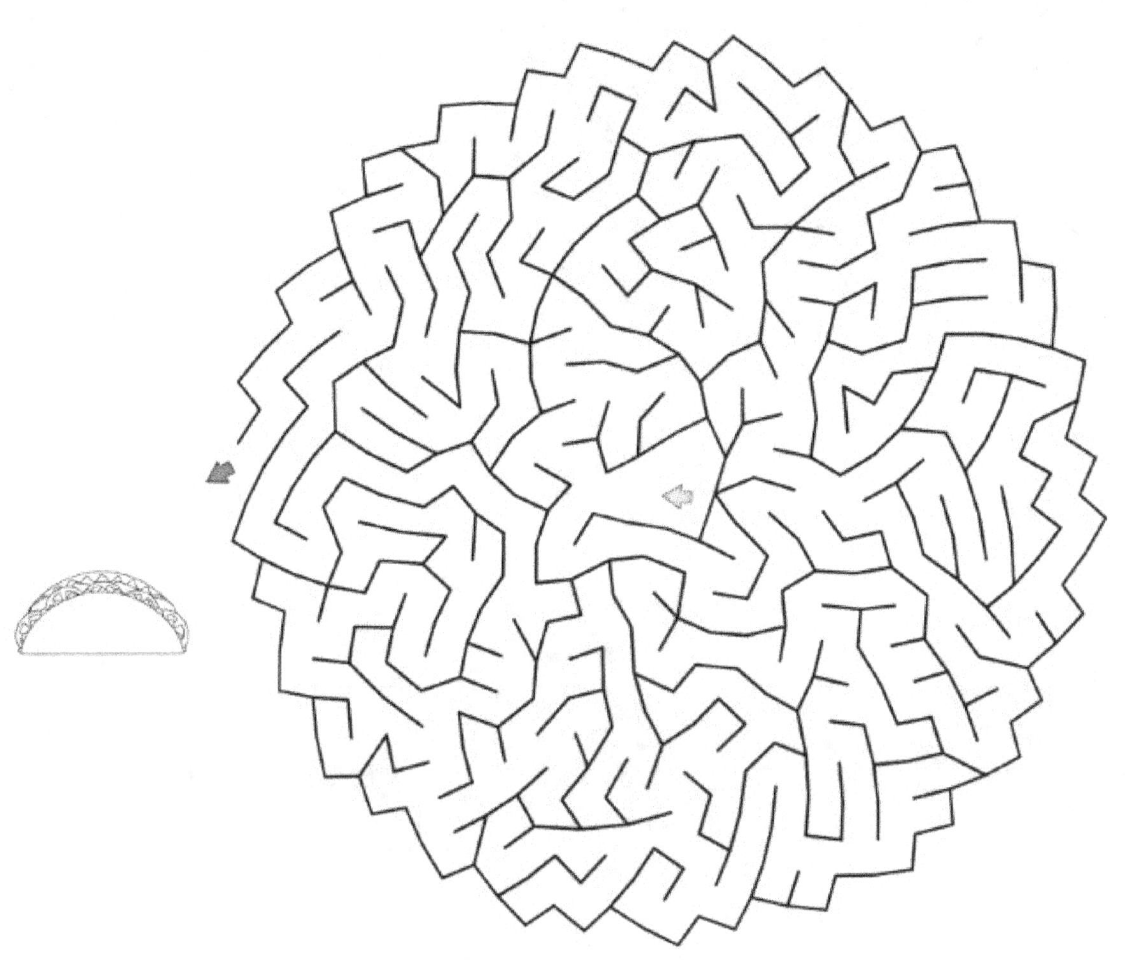

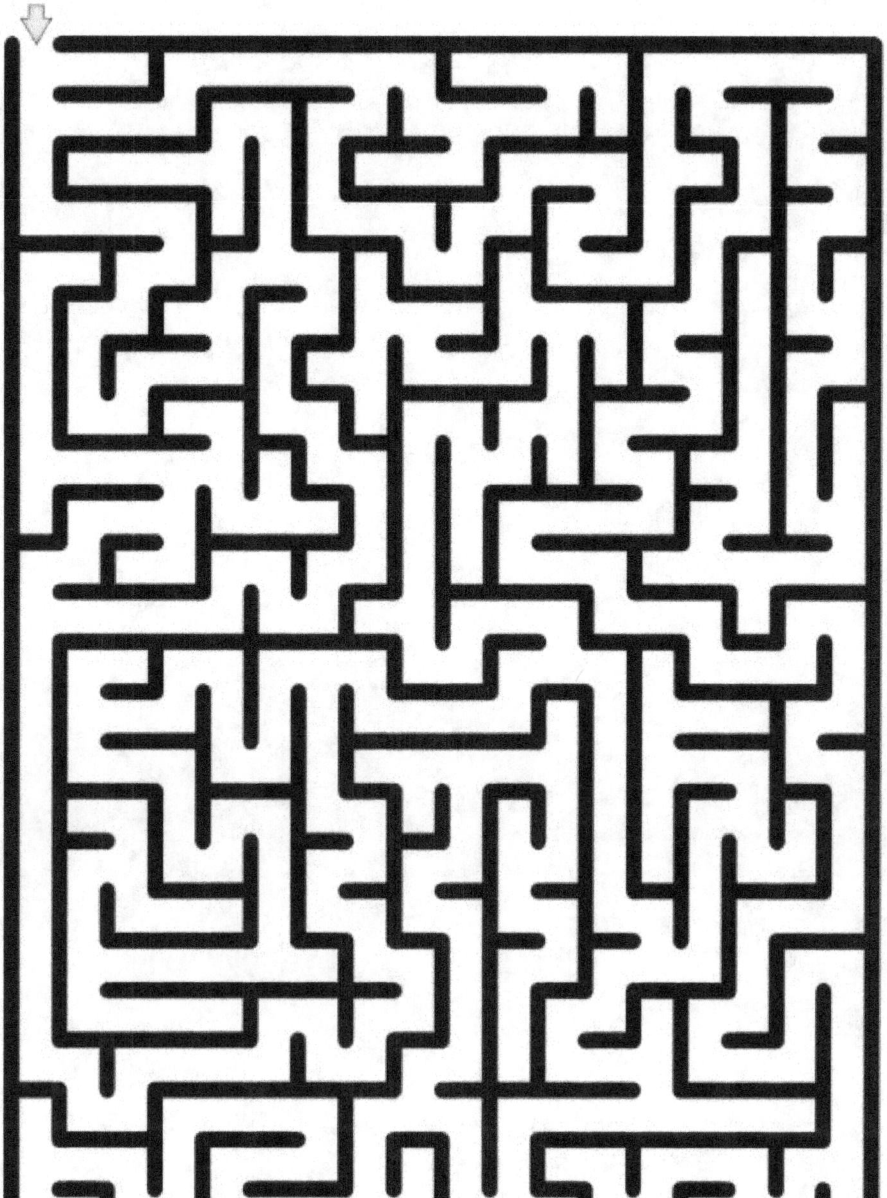

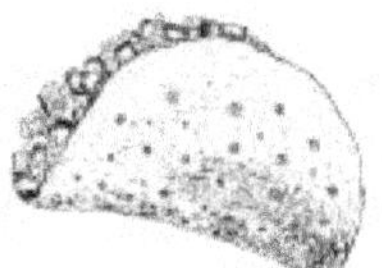

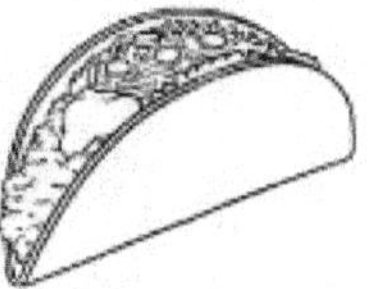

www.ingramcontent.com/pod-product-compliance
Lightning Source LLC
Chambersburg PA
CBHW081739250726
48657CB00010B/3330